VIS À VIS

Vis à Vis

FIELD NOTES ON
POETRY & WILDERNESS

DON MCKAY

WITH ILLUSTRATIONS BY
WESLEY W. BATES

GASPEREAU PRESS MMI

*C*ontents

AUTHOR'S NOTE 9

BALER TWINE 11

MATÉRIEL 35

REMEMBERING APPARATUS 51

THE CANOE PEOPLE 75

THE BUSHTITS' NEST 79

"All events fear their words"
— ELIAS CANETTI

Author's Note

These essays, and the related long poem, were written over the last decade of the twentieth century, a decade in which I was determined to come to grips with the practice of nature poetry in a time of environmental crisis. That coming to grips might be better described as a series of wrestling matches, in each of which the poet attempted to pin his vocation to the mat while avoiding the same fate himself. When the poet achieved a draw (alas, no victories), some thinking, of a rough and duct-taped variety, got done; when the vocation won he got dragged off into birdwatching, poetry, lallygagging or silence. Over the decade, the final score is something like 76–0–3 in favour of the vocation. Just the same, it seems worthwhile to preserve the drawn matches, and I am grateful to Gaspereau Press for making that possible, and in a form so sensitive to their subject, whose importance far exceeds the feints and gestures of the words.

The essays have often had their source in conversation with friends on the trail or in the kitchen. Among many, let me mention Tim Lilburn, Robert Bringhurst, Stan Dragland and Trevor Goward. Especially I have to thank Jan Zwicky for lending the companionship, fierce listening and editorial patience required for these notions to struggle into written form.

Baler Twine

THOUGHTS ON RAVENS,
HOME & NATURE POETRY

Ravens have not been common in my experience and so haven't receded into the familiar; every time I encounter one it flies more or less straight out of tricksterhood and the legends of Haida culture. It arrives like a brash postcard from the wilderness, and the impulse to respond is strong. Mind you, corvids — crows, ravens, jays, magpies — have often struck us this way: as talkers, as folk philosophers and tricksters whose curiosity is mixed with skepticism to produce that particular quality of canniness and mordant humour. Along a wilderness trail you expect ravens to check you out and extract what they can from your food, and to discuss your (sloppy) campcraft hoarsely and at length from the top of a nearby pine. Last winter two ravens, whom I mistook for a blown-away umbrella, appeared on my feeder, covering it completely. On Yellowknife's golf course, I hear, there is a ground rule covering the possibility of a raven stealing your ball. (Should that, I wonder, constitute a penalty or a bonus? Let's say that if a raven steals your ball you have to quit playing and caddy for someone else, but take every opportunity to disrupt play, dropping the club bag as the backswing reaches its zenith, or declaiming lewd limericks based on putter and mashie. OK, but if you find a raven's feather and wear it in your hat for at least six holes, every golfer must buy you a drink afterward. Then, once you have drunk every drink, you must disrobe entirely, and, climbing to the top of a red pine....)

At least that one area of temperament – Droll Zone – is shared with ravens, whereas other wild species, even bears, strike us as requiring a stretch of some distance, and perhaps even metamorphosis, before communication is possible. In his fascinating book *Ravens in Winter*, Bernd Heinrich details the "altruistic" behaviour of ravens (and incidentally reveals his own devotion and endurance as an observer), establishing that they will frequently alert one another to the presence of carcasses, research which creates problems for "hard" evolutionary theory. To the rest of us whose acquaintance is more casual, ravens, like otters, seem to venture three-fifths of the way into anthropomorphosis on their own; perhaps this is why, whenever I see one, I feel absurdly gregarious, and often find myself croaking back, hoping it might decide to perch a spell. Yes, there's a kind of reverence in this. I do imagine receiving wisdom from this creature, but not packaged as wisdom. It'll come dressed as talk, palaver. And it will have conten — unlike, say, the pure lyric of a white-throated sparrow.

The first time I saw ravens up close was some years ago in Alberta near Blue Ridge, where ten or twelve of them were playing loop-the-loop. There is a high gravel bank on one side of the river, which must have created quite a wind-bounce, because the ravens were soaring at high speed right at the bank, then, just before impact, shooting up into the air thirty feet or so. They would bail out in that characteristic tumble, clownish, deliberate boys-on-a-raft loss of control, flapping and falling to spill the wind, and fly back across the river to do it again: the aerial equivalent to an otter slide.

All this is preamble to my most troubling encounter with a raven, the one which is bothering me most, and which will set up the reflections that follow. (I promise to get to nature poetry eventually.) Having recently moved to New Brunswick from southwestern Ontario, I had more opportunity to observe ravens on a regular basis. For some reason, I found myself taking drives and walks with raven-watching as an agenda. Why? Perhaps it was all this reading and ruminating I'd been doing about the place of our species among others

— and the other. Was this mental space priming me to seek out contact with one of the few other creatures I can imagine speaking to me? I mean, this was an itch, an intuition, not a sacred quest or totem animal rite. Anyhow, I was driving a bit south of Gagetown along the Saint John River, where there are lots of high places to park and scan the low-lying interval land (areas which are under water during the spring flood) for large passerines. It was mid-January, quite cold, and clear. Saw a couple of ravens, far off, who were buzzing and bugging one another — romantically? (I imagine a raven relationship, which lasts a lifetime, involves a certain amount of teasing.) Saw some snow buntings, lifting off from roadside gravel like an old black and white eight-millimetre movie, flickering over a fence into a field. Then, on my way back home, I got my best look at a raven. It was hung up by the roadside at the entrance to a lane, a piece of baler twine around one leg, wings spread. There was a huge shotgun hole in its back just above the tail, which was missing altogether.

What do you think I should make of this? It won't do to be sentimental here. But this doesn't fall into an ethic of hunting; nor can it be understood from the rational-cum-aesthetic perspective of someone like Audubon, who would shoot individuals of a species in order to have tractable models. Even without the myths which attend this creature, even discounting "the sacred" and setting aside the ancient mariner, this seems very bad. Shooting the raven was one thing: we all know, each of us, that sinister delight in casual brutality and long-distance death. Displaying it was another – controlling its death, as well as taking its life. Displaying it declares that the appropriation is total. A dead body seeks to rejoin the elements; this one is required to function as a sign, a human category – a sign which simply says "we can do this." The raven's being, in Martin Heidegger's terms, was not just used, but used up.

So I cut it down. Its wings were large and eloquent, and not like anything I could think of, certainly not like blown-away umbrellas. The feathers, including the lavish neck-flounce, were still very glossy and fine. Its eyes were sphincters of nothing. And where did I get that notion that black was "merely" the absence of colour?

Now I'd like to freeze me there, standing by the road with a dead raven on a piece of baler twine, wondering what to do with it, while we consider some of the reading and reflection I mentioned. We might think of this as climbing a ladder of o's into a thought-balloon above my head, where a small flock of issues awaits. To reduce the cacophony, I'll try voicing these one at a time, but let's keep in mind that this is not a necessary or logical progression.

MATÉRIEL

What happened to the raven is I think an example of one pole of our relations to material existence, which I have come to call "matériel." In its limited sense matériel is military equipment; in a slightly larger sense it is any equipment owned by an institution. But I'm taking the term to apply even more widely to any instance of second-order appropriation, where the first appropriation is the making of tool, or the address to things in the mode of utility, the mindset which Heidegger calls "standing reserve." To make things into tools in the first place, we remove them from autonomous existence and conscript them as servants, determining their immediate futures. To make tools into matériel, we engage in a further appropriation. This second appropriation of matter may be the colonization of its death, as in the case of the raven, the nuclear test site, the corpse hung on a gibbet or public crucifixion. On the other hand, matérielization could be a denial of death altogether, as in the case of things made permanent and denied access to decomposition, their return to elements. We inflict our rage for immortality on things, marooning them on static islands;

and then, frequently enough, we condemn them as pollutants. Why are the fixed smiles on Barbie Dolls and Fisher Price toys so pathetic?

WILDERNESS

By "wilderness" I want to mean, not just a set of endangered spaces, but the capacity of all things to elude the mind's appropriations. That tools retain a vestige of wilderness is especially evident when we think of their existence in time and eventual graduation from utility: breakdown. To what *degree* do we own our houses, hammers, dogs? Beyond that line lies wilderness. We probably experience its presence most often in the negative as dry rot in the basement, a splintered handle, or shit on the carpet. But there is also the sudden angle of perception, the phenomenal surprise which constitutes the sharpened moments of *haiku* and imagism. The coat hanger asks a question; the armchair is suddenly crouched: in such defamiliarizations, often arranged by art, we encounter the momentary circumvention of the mind's categories to glimpse some thing's autonomy — its rawness, its *duende*, its alien being.

HOME

Omphalos, Ithaca, genesis, and telos: "home" is so interwoven with "human" that it tends to function, in most humanistic art, as the fundamental and unquestioned category, underlying all other motives, even romantic love. One way to set it, a little, at a distance, is to come at it from the vantage point of the phenomenology of the other. Home, we may say, is the action of the inner life finding outer form; it is the settling of self into the world. As such, it makes the first appropriation, the fundamental move that possesses the other; the hand grasps the thing and removes it from its element, relieving it of its autonomy and anonymity: the thing is both owned and named. In Emmanuel Levinas' philosophy, this grasping is a signal event, for his account of consciousness does not begin with a stable I but with the other, out of which "I" coagulates through a process of recollection and representation. The self is "made of" the other, and is not a pre-existing container in which the other is registered. "Home," in such a mode of thinking, is an important development because it substantiates the self (even a name, John Berger points out, is a home in a minimal sense) and separates it from the world. It establishes the *place* where representation and recollection occur, and breaks the plenum of experience.

Before the establishment of home, the hand related to things sensuously through the caress, but it is with the "primordial grasp," as Levinas calls it, that possession, including knowledge, begins. Home makes possible the possession of the world, the rendering of the other as one's interior.

It might seem that home is the moment of passage from ontological to epistemological dwelling, the place where knowledge as power begins. But this needs to be balanced with our intuitive sense that home is also the site of our appreciation of the material world, where we lavish attention on its details, where we collaborate with it. In fact, it often seems that home, far from being just a concretization of self, is the place where it pours itself out into the world, interiority opening itself to material expression. To make a home is to establish identity with a primordial grasp, yes; but it is also, in some measure, to give it away with an extended palm. We might try to sum up the paradox of home-making by saying that inner life *takes place*: it both *claims* place and acts to *become* a place among others. It turns wilderness into an interior and presents interiority to the wilderness.

Inside humanistic thinking, as well, it is often useful to construe home as a crossing place, an intersection of axes. John Berger, developing an idea of Mircea Eliade's, sees home as the place where, at least until our century, the world could be founded and made sense of, the heart of the real.

> Home was the centre of the world because it was the place where a vertical line crossed with a horizontal one. The vertical line was a path leading upwards to the sky and downwards to the underworld. The horizontal line represented the traffic of the world, all the possible roads leading across the earth to other places. Thus, at home, one was nearest to the gods in the sky and to the dead in the underworld. This nearness promised access to both. And at the same time, one was at the starting point and, hopefully, the returning point of all terrestrial journeys.

When the human project becomes inscribed on and in the world, the right angle appears, this sign of intersecting axes, the twofold which is at once paradoxical (and so gestures to multiplicity) and reductive (the simplification of a manifold to a polarity). Human dwelling is essentially *constructed*, carpentered. In the wilderness one's vision is enriched by abundant curvilinear forms, but it is also threatened by them. There is a genuine relief and assurance in the taut lines of the tent, the crisp angles of a bridge, a road, even — if mildly lost — a powerline cut. As Paul Shepard has observed, our strong preference for landforms that seem to mimic our architecture is reflected in their designation as parks ("National Monuments" is the significant American term), a sort of canonization of selected sites that approximate the terms of human, angled, dwelling. There are plenty of mythological reasons for having cemeteries full of crosses and tombstones, but we should also be alive to the pure propriety of the visual gesture: the dead are leaving the constructed world of right angles, and their exit is crowded with them — joints, ledgers, sills, doorways into dissolution. Not to mention the pathos of the coffin itself: the last room, delivered with its body into process. With this gesture, we relinquish the notion of home, along with that peculiarly, though not exclusively, human idea of an existence apart from wilderness.

POETIC ATTENTION
& THE AEOLIAN HARP

Admitting that you are a nature poet, nowadays, may make you seem something of a fool, as though you'd owned up to being a Sunday painter at, say, the Nova Scotia College of Art and Design. There are some valid reasons for this. At present, "nature" has been so lavishly oversold that the word immediately invokes several kinds of vacuous piety, ranging from Rin-tin-tinism to knee-jerk environmental concerns. "Nature," with its secular term, "the environment," constitutes that portion of television that is not news, weather, serial drama, sports, or sitcoms, a sort of documentary melodrama which fuses spectacle with sentimentality. It has been, as someone quipped, Lorne Greened.

The first indicator of one's status as nature poet is that one does not invoke language right off when talking about poetry, but acknowledges some extra-linguistic condition as the poem's input, output, or both. A second indicator may be actual content, front lawn to back country, but this, if one uses my peculiar notion of wilderness; becomes a dubious signal, since the poet may be focussed on the wilderness in a car, a coat hanger, or even language itself, as much as Kluane Park. (She might, in point of fact, be focussed on Kluane Park as a tool.) My own reasons for failing to postmodernize are merely empirical: before, under, and through the wonderful terrible wrestling with words and music there is a state of mind which I'm calling "poetic attention." I'm calling it that, though even as I name it I can feel the falsity (and in some way the transgression) of nomination: it's a sort of readiness, a species of longing which is without the desire to possess, and it does not really wish to be talked about. To me, this is a form of knowing which counters the "primordial grasp" in home-making, and celebrates the wilderness of the other; it gives ontological applause. Even after linguistic composition has begun, and the air is thick with the problematics of reference, this kind of knowing remains in touch with perception. The nature poet may (should, in fact) resort to the field guide or library, but will keep coming, back, figuratively speaking, to the trail — to the grain of the experience, the particular angle of expression in a face, and okay, to the raven on the baler twine.

There is, for this nature poet, at any rate, an important distinction between poetic attention and romantic inspiration. The romantic poet (or tourist, for that matter) desires to be spoken *to*, inspired by the other, so that perception travels into language (or slide show) without a palpable break. The paradigm for this ideal relation is the aeolian harp, which is simply the larynx of natural phenomena, "Sensations sweet / felt in the blood, and felt along the heart / And passing even into my purer mind." Or it may be that poetry itself is seen as natural, as in Neruda's

> And it was at that age ... Poetry
> arrived in search of me. I don't know,
> I don't know where it came from, from
> winter or a river.

Wonderful: we want to believe this graceful act of personification and animism; why should it not be true, as music, or as fairytale is? Aeolian harpism relieves us of our loneliness as a species, reconnects us to the natural world, restores a coherent reality. It also, not incidentally, converts natural energy into imaginative power, so that Romanticism, which begins in the contemplation of nature, ends in the celebration of the creative imagination in and for itself. No wonder it is so compelling, whether we find it in Wordsworth, Neruda, or Levertov: it speaks directly to a deep and almost irresistible desire for unity. But poetic attention is based on a recognition and a valuing of the other's wilderness; it leads to a work which is not a *vestige* of the other, but a *translation* of it.

OBJECTION & RESPONSE

Enter the ambassador from post-structural theory. "Well, this is all very well, Mr. Nature Poet, standing by the roadside, outfitted no doubt by L. L. Bean, happily twirling your dead raven, but it's a fact that you're going to crash into language in about .05 seconds, and that your perception is already saturated with it. This parade of perceptual innocence is simply a new twist on the old notion of romantic inspiration, designed to sneak a transcendental signified back into the game. Before you ever came upon the dead raven your head was filled with myths and soft ecology, a whole library of assumptions about the 'natural' world, as you yourself acknowledged in your charming, anecdotal, introduction. The individual who stands and stares at the dead raven or live warbler, ontologically applauding, is always already made of linguistic and cultural categories, loosely strung together, in your case, with the mental equivalent of baler twine. The nature poet, like anyone else, is 'locked in a tower of words' as Dylan Thomas puts it; imagining otherwise is romantic mysticism. Need I go on?"

Putting aside for the moment the question of whether non-linguistic experience is possible (whether there may be an element of wilderness in perception), let me acknowledge the force of this objection. Given the unique relation of language to our species, how can our perception, as well as our writing, *not* be a restructuring of the world? Nature poetry's paradoxical situation is, I think, roughly analogous to home-making. Being language, it cannot avoid the primordial grasp, but this occurs simultaneously with the extended palm, the openness in knowing that I've been calling poetic attention. And that experience suggests strongly that, although it cannot be spoken, radical otherness exists. In fact, nature poetry should not be taken to be *avoiding* anthropocentrism, but to be enacting it, thoughtfully. It performs the translation which is at the heart of being human, the simultaneous grasp and gift of home-making. And the persistence of poetic attention during the act of composition is akin to the translator's attention to the original, all the while she performs upon it a delicate and dangerous transformation. Our epistemological dilemma is not resolved, as by aeolian harpism, but ritualized and explored.

The ambassador from post-structuralism has also done us a service by pointing out that the step-by-step model of perception-translation is too simple and naive. Language *is* already there in poetic attention; like an athlete at her limit, language is experiencing its speechlessness and the consequent need to stretch *itself* to be adequate to this form of knowing. Part of the excitement inside this species of meditative act is linguistic; it's the excitement of a tool which has hatched the illicit desire to behave like an animal.

One word more on post-structural thought: in its problematization of terms like "nature" and "natural" (that is, in their reduction to disguised categories of language and culture) it provides a salutary check on romantic innocence, a positive reminder of the fact of the frame. But — and here I indulge in intuition based on tone and style — its skepticism nurtures its excess, secretly worships a nihilistic impulse as surely as Romanticism worshipped the creative imagination in the guise of nature. It is, no less than Romanticism, an ideology, a politics, and an erotics, despite protestations to the contrary. In the realm of ideas, as in human relations, we do well to suspect any basic drive that presents itself simply as method or a form of rationalism. That is, to be blunt, it is as dangerous to act as though we were not a part of nature as it is to act as though we were not a part of culture; and the intellectual and political distortions produced by these contrary ideologies are greatly to be feared.

❧

Imagine: a trail made of moments rather than minutes, wild bits of time which resist elapsing according to a schedule. Pauses. Each one bell-shaped, into which you step as an applicant for the position of tongue. Or: each pause is designed as the unbuilt dwelling of that moment — a cabin, a stanza, a gazebo, a frame — a room which the trail accepts as a fiction or wish. This is the point of anthropomorphic play, the erotic hinge of translation. When ownership is set aside, appropriation can turn inside out, an opening, a way of going up to something with a gift from home. Growths on this stump remind you that the Japanese call certain fungi "tree ears"; the red pine around them are a ceremonial parade for Moustache Day; you see ravens playing on the Athabaska River and think "boys on a raft." Anthropomorphic play, along this trail, is a gift to the other from the dwelling you will never build there. How? A slight deformation of human categories, an extra metaphorical stretch and silliness of language as it moves toward the other, dreaming its body. There is danger in this gift, because language, in this poetic mode, compromises its nature, dismantling itself in a gesture toward wilderness. "The inverse of language," says Emmanuel Levinas, "is like a laughter that seeks to destroy language, a laughter infinitely reverberated." Poets are supremely interested in what language can't do; in order to gesture outside, they use language in a way that flirts with its destruction. Language wears tree ears and a false moustache for the moment. For whom? For the *moment*.

Meanwhile I am still standing by the roadside dangling a dead raven, wondering what to do. When we were kids, dead birds were a fine opportunity for funerals; we'd bury them in shoe boxes and get in on this *death* business, fool around with the magic of ritual — candles, solemnity, shredded pansies. The sparrow, needless to say, had become the excuse for the sentimental carnival we cooked up; we didn't need romantic poets to tell us about converting natural into imaginative energy. Might some more chaste and adult ritual work here? Although I am reluctant to dismiss the value of ritual gestures — especially those grown within a culture that lives more comfortably on the hinge of translation — no such act suggests itself to me at this place and time. It is January, remember, so even a quick burial would be tough work; I don't have a shovel with me; and I'm feeling conspicuous. There are hunters' rites that balance an overt act of appropriation with one of homage to the slain animal. But I doubt if these work with matériel, where the death-and-reduction comes thoughtlessly, from long distance, *delivered*, in the significant parlance of military strategists. There is no ritual imaginable which would, right now, set in balance our relation to Pacific atolls blown up in hydrogen bomb tests, or to clear-cut forests, or to the ecosphere itself. Just find a hollow for the raven where no one is likely to find it; cover it with brush so that it may decompose in private; drive away; think; read. There is imaginative work to be done.

Matériel

1. THE MAN FROM NOD

Since his later history is so obscure, it's no wonder he is most remembered for his first bold steps in the areas of sibling rivalry and land use. It should not be forgotten that, although Adam received God's breath, and angels delivered his message, it was Cain who got tattooed – inscribed with the sign which guarantees a sevenfold revenge to be dished out to antagonists. Sometimes translated "Born to Lose."

He was the first to realize there is no future in farming.

How must he have felt, after tilling, sowing, weeding, harvesting, and finally offering his crop, about God's preference for meat? Was God trying to push his prized human creatures further into the fanged romance of chasing and escaping? Was he already in the pocket of the cattle barons? Cain must have scratched and scratched his head before he bashed in his brother's.

He becomes the first displaced person, exiled to the land of Nod, whose etymology, as he probably realized, was already infected with wandering. Then his biography goes underground, rumouring everywhere. Some say he tries farming once again in the hinterland, scratching illegibly at the glacial till before hitting the first road. Some say he fathers a particularly warlike tribe, the Kenites. Some, like Saint Augustine, claim that he takes revenge on agriculture by founding the first cities, rationalizing all his wanderings into streets and tenements, and so charting the course for enclosures and clearances to come. But perhaps his strategy is simpler and more elegant. Perhaps he just thins into his anger, living as a virus in the body politic: the wronged assassin, the antifarmer, the terrorist tattooed with the promise of sevenfold revenge. Like anyone, he wants to leave his mark.

2. FATES WORSE THAN DEATH

Atrocity
implies an audience of gods.
The gods watched as swiftfooted
godlike Achilles cut behind the tendons of both feet
and pulled a strap of oxhide through
so he could drag the body of Hektor,
tamer of horses, head down in the dust
behind his chariot.
Some were appalled, some not,
having nursed their grudges well, until
those grudges were fine milkfed
adolescents, armed
with automatic weapons. The gods,
and farther off,
the gods before the gods, those who ate
their children and contrived
exquisite tortures in eternity, watched
and knew themselves undead. Such is the loss, such
the wrath of swiftfooted godlike
Achilles, the dumb fucker, that he drags,
up and down, and round and round the tomb
of his beloved, the body of Hektor,
tamer of horses. Atrocity

is never senseless. No. Atrocity is dead ones
locked in sense, forbidden
to return to dust, but scribbled in it,
so that everyone — the gods,
the gods before the gods, the enemy, the absent mothers, all
must read what it is like to live out exile on earth
without it, to be without recesses, place,
a campsite where the river opens
into the lake, must read
what it means to live against the sun and not to die.
Watch,
he says, alone in the public
newscast of his torment, as he
cuts behind the tendons of both feet,
and pulls a strap of oxhide through,
so that he can drag the body that cannot stop being Hektor,
tamer of horses, head down in the dust
behind his chariot, watch
this.

3. THE BASE

Unheard helicopter chop
locks my mind in neutral.
What was it I was supposed to think
as I entered the forbidden country of the base? For this
was not the wisdom I had bargained for —
banality. No orchids of evil
thriving on the phosphorus that leaks
from unexploded shells. No litter of black
ratatats like insoluble hailstones, or fungi
springing up from dead kabooms.
After nearly forty years of shattered air, I find
not one crystal in the khaki gravel.
Nondescription.

What was Cain thinking
as he wandered here? Whatever
"here" may be, for it has largely been forgotten
by the maps, and also by itself, a large anonymous
amnesia in the middle of New Brunswick.
What shapes occupied the mind
which since has occupied the landscape?
Did he foresee this triumph of enchantment
whereby place itself becomes its camouflage,

surrenders Petersville, Coot Hill and New
Jerusalem, to take up orders?
Did he anticipate the kingdom of pure policy,
whose only citizens — apart
from coyotes, ravens, moose —
are its police?
Except for graveyards, which have been
preserved, this real estate is wholly owned
and operated by the will, clearcut,
chemicalled and bombed.
Black wires like illegible writing
left everywhere. Ballistics? Baker Dog Charley?
Plastic vials tied to trees at intervals, containing
unknown viscous liquid. In some folktale
I can't conjure, I would steal this potion
and confer great gifts — or possibly destruction —
upon humanity. In a myth
or Wonderland, I'd drink it and become
a native. No thanks.
       Yet blueberries grow, creeks
sparkle, and an early robin
sings from the scrub. Can a person eat
the berries when they ripen? What kind of fish
thicken in the creeks? During hunting season,
claims the Base Commander, moose and deer
take sanctuary in the impact areas, since no personnel

may enter. Often, late September, you may
see a moose, Jean Paul L'Orignal, perhaps,
sitting on a stump along the border of the base,
huge chin resting on a foreleg,
pondering alternatives: cheerful psychopaths
in psychedelic orange, or a moose-sized replica
of the absurd, kaboom?

Now I recall
the story of the soldier detailed to attack
an "enemy position," which turned out to be
his grandfather's old farmhouse. Basic Training:
once out of nature he was not about
to get sucked in by some natural seduction
and disgrace himself with tears
or running to the kitchen for an oatmeal cookie.
He made, as we all do, an adjustment.
      Standing here
still parked in neutral
I'm unable to identify the enemy's position or
sort the evil genii from fallen
farmers, victims and assassins
interpenetrate with vendors and *vendus* in long
chromosomal threads.
      Time to retreat.
Walking back, I try to jump a creek

and sprain my wrist. Pick up your god-damned
feet –. Still, I stop to cut two
pussy willow branches. Why? Imagined
anti-fasces? Never
was the heaviness of gesture
heavier, nor hope more of a lump,
than trying to imagine that those buds
might, back home in the kitchen, unclench, each fragile hair
pom-pommed with pollen, some day
to open into leaf.

4. STRETTO

Having oversold the spirit, having,
having talked too much of angels, the fool's rush, having the wish,
thicker than a donkey's penis,
holier than o, having the wish
to dress up like the birds,
to dress up like the birds and be and be and be.
Off the hook.
Too good for the world.
Unavailable for comment.
Elsewhere.

                    Wonderful Elsewhere, Unspoiled,
Elsewhere as Advertised, Enchanted, Pristine,
Expensive. To lift, voluptuous, each feather cloak
worth fifty thousand finches: to transcend
the food chains we have perched upon and hover – hi there
fans from coast to coast – to beam back dazzling
shots of the stadium, drifting in its cosmos
like a supernova, everywhere the charged
particles of stardom winking and twinkling, o, exponentially
us. As every angel is.

                Every angel is incestuous.
Agglutinoglomerosis: The inlet choked with algae thriving on the warmth
imparted by the effluent. *Contermitaminoma*: runoff through
the clearcut takes the topsoil to the river then
out into the bay to coat the coral reef in silt. *Gagaligogo*:
seepage from the landfill finds the water table. *Elugelah*: the south-
sea island angelized by the first H-blast.
                                        In the dead sea
we will float as stones. Unmortal.

     Unmortality Incorporated.
No shadow. All day
it is noon it is no one. All day
it utters one true sentence jammed
into its period. Nothing is to be allowed
to die but everything gets killed
and then reclassified: the death of its death
makes it an art form. Hang it.
Prohibit the ravens. Prohibit the coyotes.
Prohibit the women with their oils and cloths and
weep weep weeping. Tattoo this extra letter
on the air:
  This is what we can do.
Detonation. Heartbeats of the other,
signed, sealed,
delivered. Thunder
eats of its echo eats its vowels smothers its
elf. To strike
hour after hour the same hour. To dig
redig the gravels that are no one's grave.

Gravels, aye, tis gravels ye'll gnash mit muchas gracias and will it please thee sergeant dear to boot me arse until I hear the mermaids sinking? You know it: tis the gravel of old rocknroll highroad, me darling sibs, the yellow brick jornada del muerto. You fancy me far from your minds, wandering lonely as a clod in longlost brotherhood, while your door's locked and your life's grammatically insured, yet (listen) *scurry scurry* (Is–that–Only–A–Rat–In–The–Basement–Better–Phone–Dad–Oh–No–The–Line's–Dead, Mandatory Lightning Flash) yup, here I am with the hook old chum. Hardly fair, what? Now gnash this: beautiful tooth, tooth beautiful. Repeat: die nacht ist die nacht. How many fucking times do I have to *Fucking* tell you, me rosasharns? Nayther frahlicher ner mumbo, nayther oft when on my couch I lie nor *bonny doom* will lift from off these eyes of thine their click clock particles of record time. *Ammo ergo somme.* We bombs it back to square one, then, o babes in arms, we bombs square one. Nomine Fat Boy ate Elugelah ate Alamogordo gravel. Mit click clock lock licht nicht.
Encore.
Die Nacht ist die Nacht.

Remembering Apparatus

POETRY AND THE
VISIBILITY OF TOOLS

$\mathcal{R}$ecently I held a yard sale because I wanted to convert clutter into money. I advertised in the paper, emphasizing the range of articles for sale — furniture, books, clothing, appliances, household items. I put up posters at the university which hinted that Real Finds swam like pike among the weeds, that this was a place where, not only might a useful pre-owned chair be acquired, but an *objet* might be *trouvé*. On Friday I began lugging stuff from the basement and contriving its artful display on planks laid between boxes and that old set of speakers (themselves on sale) in the yard and garage, enjoying the twin pleasures of spring cleaning and junior capitalism, spiced with a dash of gypsy *élan*. But these mainstream yard sale feelings were followed by a mood that surprised me. Once out of storage and onto the lawn, the clutter looked different: each thing emerged from the general mess into its own identity. It was as though the monetary concern (how much can I ask for a dysfunctional Lawnboy?) triggered a wider sense of value, one that had to do with our connection and shared experience (lotta grass through the old blade, eh?) over the years. Walter Benjamin claims that ownership is the most intimate relation we can have with things; but I wonder if that intimacy is not, like marriage, shadowed by familiarity's dead hand. Of course Benjamin is thinking of connoisseurship, but I have it on good report that a painting or a first edition can become as invisible as a kettle.

But besides the defamiliarizing effect of lawn and garage — which were taking on, so I hoped, something of a carnival air — there was the fact of my gesture in putting these possessions up for sale. Now that they were on waivers, the portable typewriter and the fifties floorlamp, the royal wedding souvenir plate and the lacrosse sticks, stood firmly etched, separate from my motives and needs. Almost all of them were, using the term broadly, tools; but tools whose usefulness to me was finished. And the very lack which had condemned them to the yard sale now nudged them a few degrees in the direction of art, that class of objects which are eloquent and useless. Normally this phase of Yard Sale Mind would be confined to the brief period between assembly and first sale. But in my case it had lots of time to swell to a major theme, since Saturday afternoon brought first rain, which dampened the serendipitous, gossipy curiosity which yard sales satisfy, then snow, which froze it. Springtime in

New Brunswick. I had plenty of time to sit in the garage, door shut tight against the wind, wearing the jacket I had been willing to let go for five dollars. Declarations made during the lugging phase hung in the air — declarations to the effect that this was a one-way street and unsold items would be moving to the Salvation Army, not back to the expletive deleted basement. Only a few grim yard salers appeared. I hoped no one wanted to buy the old electric heater, whose usefulness, after all, was not quite dead.

The invisibility of tools: pieces of equipment, as Martin Heidegger observes, are used up in their equipmentality, unlike works of art. This attitude — or lack of attitude — to constructed things stems from our easy assumption that a definition of things under the heading of utility is adequate, that their being is fully explained by what they're used for. It may take some break in the surface of experience — a failed yard sale or accident — for us to see that tools exceed the fact of their construction and exemplify an otherness beyond human design. The wilderness is not just far away and dwindling, but implicit in things we use every day, as close at hand as a flat tire or a missed step. It is one function of art to provide safe defamiliarizing moments, when the mask of utility gets lifted and we waken to that residual wilderness without the inconvenience of breakdown or disaster.

No less than the 'simple' tools in my garage, digital technology tends to become invisible. It is not hard to find evidence for the claim (Heidegger's, again) that invisibility is part of technology's essence, as fundamental to its power as the benefits it bestows. When slow and suspicious people offer resistance to the spread of computers, they are often mollified (after various threats concerning competition in the marketplace and job security have been levied) with the expression 'it's just a tool'. We could do worse than consult Marshall McLuhan to rebut this empty assurance since, amoral though his prophecies may seem, they leave us in little doubt about tool use at this level.

> Man becomes as it were the sex organ of the machine world, as the bee of the plant world, enabling it to fecundate and to evolve ever new forms. The machine world reciprocates man's love by expediting his wishes and desires, namely by providing him with wealth.
>
> (*Understanding Media*)

In *Rogue Primate*, J. L. Livingston assesses our species from an evolutionary and broadly environmental perspective (and without McLuhan's cheeriness): we are the domesticating species that has domesticated *itself* to technology; we inhabit it, we live by its requirements, and we tailor our lives to suit them. At a certain level of dependence the power shifts in the relation between user and tool. We become, in Arthur Kroker's memorable phrase, data trash.

Meanwhile, back in my garage, I am musing along the shelf of handy household items. When my parents moved into a condo, they had the usual accumulation to dispose of, including this old metal meat-grinder — the kind that clamps onto the kitchen counter, with a hole in the top, an auger in the middle, and a set of different plates that screw on the exit end to regulate the consistency of the product. It looks like a fossil from the Burgess Shale, or a relic from the inquisition, and I recall how, when it was taken down from the cupboard and screwed onto the counter, the kitchen took a step back toward the butcher shop and sideways into the exotic. The handle hung like a trunk, just begging to be turned. Sometimes we got to work it, pushing chunks of stewing meat in the top, feeling the auger grab and stuff them inexorably through the holes. I don't recall thinking then — as I do now, weighing this prehistoric item in my hand — that this was an extension of the abattoir, stuffing the animal through the machine. But I do recall that thrill of *tabu* and open carnality surfacing in the meticulous kitchen. If you're a vegetarian, wondering if this tool will work to grind beans, I can tell you that it won't (something I neglected to mention to the woman who paused over it, earlier in the day when the yard sale was still something of a business venture, to remark that these things still work better for some jobs than a food processor). The beans are too slippery, I think.

The meat-grinder is more visible than the food processor. On the one hand its operations are open, and involve us in actual work; on the other, its own *madeness* is entirely evident. For that connectedness to the material world and physical action, that residual wilderness in tools, I'm reserving the term *apparatus* as a way of seeing tools and technology a little more complexly. Whereas the meat-grinder wears its apparatus-nature, the computer hides, and seeks to reside wholly in utility — *just* a tool, as it were. That is not to say we can't construe digital technology as apparatus, but that it requires more effort, since those operations which make possible the storage, transmission, and retrieval of immense amounts of information have already been performed by designers and programmers, some of whom may be other computers. There are millions of 'apparatus actions' behind and before the calling-up of your bank record to the screen, which involve the translation of all the thought processes required for any task into a series of binary alternatives. Such work is much closer to the meat-grinder than it is to the easy, elegant world sold to consumers by virtual realtors. Ellen Ullman, a former program designer, speaks of this out of her experience:

> The problem with programming is not that the computer is illogical – the computer is terribly logical, relentlessly literal. It demands that the programmer explain the world on its terms; that is, as an algorithm that must be written down in order, in a specific syntax, in a strange language that is only partially readable by human beings. To program is to translate between the chaos of human life and the rational, line by line world of computer language.
>
> (*Resisting the Virtual Life*)

What I want to stress here is the remembrance of translation, the work performed in Ullman's logical sweatshop. Information – which is often presented as essence, 'raw' material – is actually the equivalent of plastic produced in a lab, and may be just as resistant to breakdown into elements. To remember translation, recalling the apparatus-nature of digital technology, would be a check on its tendency (one wants to say *desire*) to re-combine, to produce meta- upon meta-system until it reaches the exhilarating, vertiginous world of cyberspace. But even bringing it up I feel like Friar Lawrence addressing Romeo and Juliet about the virtues of chastity; we can all sense that huge urge to forget, that pull like an eroticized amnesia to jack in and be nourished, embraced, informed. Why would McLuhan's sexual insects want to mess up their pleasurable symbiosis? And I suspect that this pull is so powerful because it is the return of an earlier forgetfulness of translation — one that was even more compelling, more erotic, and even more immense in terms of what was lost in translation: that is, forgetfulness of the translation into language itself. In fact, it has become orthodox to doubt — at least in the seminar room — that there is a world which precedes or exists outside the text.

To think of language as apparatus, to use and inhabit it with an awareness of residual wilderness, is to be conscious of ourselves as translators of the world, wielders of a technology that remains visible. An excellent translation does not wish to supersede the original, nor make us forget its existence. Yes, it must 're-grow' or 're-envision' the work in the receptor language; yes, a 'new work of art' is achieved when Montale is rendered into English by William Arrowsmith. But this new work remains in delicate, tense relation to the original; to succeed it must, in fact, preserve that connection through fine fibres of music and meaning, a host of small decisions covering shading and tone, measurements of exactitude and fidelity, judgements of cultural paraphrase and musical felicity. It would not be wrong to say that a translator's real power lies in her humility: and this includes not only reverence for the source, but a remembrance of language as apparatus.

By equipping us with a huge artificial memory, digital technology encourages us to forget much, including the fact of translation. But with 'natural' languages the wilderness may still be accessible. Naming is obviously *artificial*, whether we approach it through myth (Adam's task), taxonomical system, or the ordinary process of naming the baby. It may be governed by the desire for system (as with ear-tagged cattle and social insurance numbers); by historical considerations ('But there has always been a Christopher in the family', Steller's jay, Washington DC); or by an attempt to preserve, in the physique of language, the vestige of wilderness (chickadee, L'Huard, Seamus Heaney's *Anahorish*). Amateur naturalists trying to identify a plant or animal (though 'recognize' would perhaps be a better name for this familiar act) frequently experience a sort of vertigo as they stand, field guide in hand, beside a trail, registering the incommensurability of the plant's infinitude of parts, processes, and ecological relations with the tag that attaches it to language and makes it accessible to human intelligence. The small measure of congruence evident with the onomatopoeic chickadee disappears entirely with ring-necked duck, a beautiful diving duck whose neck ring is all but invisible unless you're holding the bird in your hands. Calling Native Americans 'Indians' similarly reveals the rickety apparatus of nomination. But even 'apt' names touch but a tiny portion of a creature, place, or thing. When that vertigo arrives, we're aware of the abject thinness of language, while simultaneously realizing its necessity. As with tools, it is often during such momentary breakdowns that we sense the enormous, unnameable wilderness beyond it — a wilderness we both long for and fear.

That longing, perhaps like all desire, carries within it the image of the longed-for thing; it is bewildering because it brings the wilderness, in a small way, into our inner lives. A Sartrean confronted by the same phenomenon calls the response nausea — a sea-sickness caused by the rational unaccountability of the world. But whether we know it as vertigo, bewilderment, or nausea, this is a point of crisis which must resolve into one of its elements, longing or fear; it is a peak upon which we can't live. A fearful response may lead to aggressive rationalism, and the defensive reduction of wilderness to standing reserve — its use-value. But longing: well, longing leads to poetry, which speaks out of, and sometimes to, this crisis in the naming of things. I'm going to try to address that idea in detail, but before I do, let me offer a small thought experiment to mark the significance of the moment of linguistic bewilderment, and perhaps to ease its discomfort as well. Suppose we read the trail guide *to* the creature we are regarding, as though putting on a performance of our native arts for a distinguished visitor to language. Think of the spreading dogbane or phoebe as a Martian to whom you are showing sci-fi films about its image in our culture. This would have the virtue of being both formal and absurd, and so bring the solace of ritual enactment to the great ache of our inevitable separation.

Poetry comes in here, as a function of language in its apparatus-nature, and not as its crowning glory. Poetry comes about because language is not able to represent raw experience, yet it must; it comes about because translation is only translation, apparatus is apparatus.

> Language is a hand, a hand
> used to pulling on galoshes: ribbed nails, long thumb
> that lies along a car door
> like a donkey's ear against its neck
> (Jan Zwicky, "Language is Hands")

For a long time before it becomes a speaking, Heidegger observes, poetry is only a listening. I think this listening involves hearkening both with and beyond language, in somewhat the same way a paddle attends to the river and conveys its energy to your wrist, even as it helps you across. Poets are notorious for dawdling, idling, lallygagging, woolgathering – the outward manifestations of that condition of listening into which they have retreated, taking language with them. And when poetry does become speech, it returns to the business of naming with this listening folded inside it. It introduces the unnameable (that is, wilderness under the sign of language) into nomination, with the result that all namings, including the poem in which it speaks, become provisional. To name without claiming is to wear ears on the outside of the statement.

Here, I think, we touch on the phenomenal roots of the figure known as apostrophe – the address to the subject which returns to Adam's task in a wholly different frame of mind. The 'o' which sometimes precedes apostrophe, and is always implicit in the gesture, might be described as the gawk of unknowing. In ancient Greek it is an essential grammatical ingredient, the article attending the vocative case; in poetry it is the gesture loaded with lightness, an opening into awe. It says 'this is for you, not just about you'. Apostrophe is often fastened upon if one wishes to burlesque the postures of poetry (especially among romantics of whatever octane) because it is an easily recognized feature, like the salient nose or chin on a politician. This is because that impulse to renewed address, with the genuine linguistic abjection which precipitates it, really is the radical of poetry: O cows, O leaves, O fridge, O presences, O yellow warblers.

> Harp of Osorno beneath the volcanoes
> Your dark strings sound
> the uprooting of the woods.
> (Pablo Neruda, *Still Another Day*)

Poetry always carries with it the promise of more periods of attention, more such namings, to come; it's as though Adam were to return to his task day after day, monkishly, a wanderer on the way rather than God's star pupil and protégé. It is not so much the famous raid on the inarticulate as the infection of articulation by the wilderness it normally feeds on and ignores.

Like technology in general, language becomes invisible when its necessity and ubiquity are assumed. Unless some breakdown occurs – words fail to convey the image of a duck, or are caught out preserving repressive attitudes, as with racist or sexist discourse — its systematic features work without check, without that healthy sense of the rifts of translation. Everything defers to, or depends on, or simply becomes, language.

Now it's one thing to claim that poetry springs from a desire to invoke the wilderness outside language, and another to show how this happens — how the apparatus functions, as it were. After all, isn't poetry *made* of language? How can it remind language of the other, while it clearly belongs to the technology itself? Reminders of the material body of words (onomatopoeia, *écriture féminine*) are all well and good, but they will seem mere adornments, like elaborate walnut TV consoles, or fine leather laptop cases, unless we can see the agents of apparatus working inside semantic action, inside the making of meaning itself.

Suppose, then, there was another way of making linguistic sense, something that would both escape reason and carry inescapable conviction?

> *You are my sunshine*
> *My only sunshine.*

Metaphor, and its related figures, use language's totalizing tendency against itself, making a claim for sameness which is clearly, according to common linguistic sense, false. Except that it isn't: no one needs it explained that some of the qualities of sunshine are those which characterize the singer's significant other. With a metaphor that works we're immediately convinced of the truth of the claim *because* it isn't rational. The leap always says (besides its fresh comparison) that language is not commensurate with the real, that leaps are necessary if we are to regain some sense of the world outside it. In this sense, metaphor's first act is to un-name its subject, reopening the question of reference. It's as though we were able to refer beyond reference, to use sameness against itself to bring the other, and a *sense* of the other (that is, its smell as well as its content) into the totality. Thanks to metaphor, we know more; but we also know that *we don't own what we know*. Metaphor has often been attacked as a contaminant (Locke) or taken as evidence (Nietzsche and his heirs among the post-structuralists) that knowledge is itself unstable or illusory. Such panicky responses occur when the wilderness surfaces inside the home; that is, inside the making of meaning itself.

Is there a way to bring metaphor to its own assistance here? I think that the figure of the trickster functions in a similar way in various mythologies, bringing the system's other into the system, personifying what appears to be chaos or pure chance. We might think of metaphor as the raven of language, a member of the mythological community who ensures that its tendency toward totality never succeeds. It is interesting that Paul De Man, in his celebrated essay "The Epistemology of Metaphor," speaks of "wild figuration," because it is clear that "wild" is spoken as a negative from within the precincts of safe knowing to mean unstable, indeterminate, insecure. And his own personification of metaphorical action is close enough to the trickster that the difference is eloquent.

> ... tropes are not just travellers, they tend to be smugglers and smugglers of stolen goods at that. What makes matters worse is that there is no way of finding out whether they do so with criminal intent or not.

Smuggler or trickster? One's preferred interpretive angle will depend, I guess, on whether the other of language, wilderness, is conceded legitimacy – 'recognized' in a political sense. One thinks of debates over the status of pirates, hackers, and Robin Hood, in respect to the totalities they oppose and subvert. Aren't they all, smugglers included, versions of the trickster in his historical and political manifestations?

Once perceived, the operations of metaphor and related figures are everywhere to be seen, common threads in the fabric rather than occasional adornments. As mentioned, this realization can have extreme consequences, and not only for chaste reasoners like John Locke. When, in his early writings,

Nietzsche finds truth itself to be "a moveable host of metaphors, metonomies and anthropomorphisms," and literal discourse to be in fact faded metaphor (and so 'illusory'), he reaches for his own metaphor – this seems to be chronic – to illustrate his point. Again, the figure is interesting.

> ... truths are illusions about which one has forgotten that this is what they are; metaphors which are worn out and without sensuous power; coins which have lost their pictures and now matter only as metal, no longer as coins.
>
> ("On Truth and Lies in an Extra-Moral Sense")

But to claim that coins become worn is to imply that they were, once, minted, and that there is a raw material which is neither shaped nor embossed. Nietzsche's coinage about the ubiquity of coinage points beyond its intended terminus – intra-linguistic illusion – to the wilderness outside language, the other which metaphorical action always includes by its gesture, whether it is part of the content or not.

The excitement of metaphor stems from the injection of wilderness into language; it is quick, tricky, and, as we have seen, not easily domesticated to utility. The sadness of metaphor stems from an awareness of lost things as we waken to the teeming life outside the language we inhabit. *Meta pherein*: carry across. Like all translations, it is a ferry whose passage one way always brings to mind the passage back. Even as we enjoy the prospect of arrival, the power of return is building within us, compromising the so-called flow of sense. No wonder every strong metaphor carries with it a whiff of *déjà vu*, the sense of memory regathered. It seems to invoke not just the particular remembrances but memory itself, huge and empty as a resonating gourd. Such oscillation – push foward, recoil back – interrupts the movement of the sentence; it creates *place* within the temporal rush of syntax.

What is this place inside language, inscribed by metaphor's recurrent back-and-forthing like the path to the outhouse? I think it is the nook of reverie, the listening post of poetry where we can pause for a moment and attend to wilderness outside the sentence we're in the middle of; the making of meaning encounters loop, encounters pool; sediment collects and settles. And among the truths which may happen there, this: a sudden awareness of the sentence itself as apparatus – a constructed, somewhat rickety tool working away at an impossible task.

Well, most often a person will go find that nook of reverie — a cabin, or a corner, or a chair — that seems conducive to composition because, like metaphor within the sentence, it's off to one side of the normal traffic of events. But sometimes the nook finds you. You miss a flight connection; the doctor is running late; or, as in my case, the yard sale gets snowed out. In some way I will always be sitting in that garage hefting the meat grinder, no longer in residence and not yet gone, my useless possessions displayed around me, and my assumptions about them in the air. The bar on the old heater is glowing. I'm wearing the jacket whose elbow I ripped during our last move, and remembering how the fifties floor lamp lit up corners of this basement apartment and that walk-up, while I wolfed down Faulkner by the riverine, fingered, hyperextended clause. I think this pause is a small retreat from language inside language, where we can sit, surrounded by our hardworking tools, exhilarated and heartbroken.

The Canoe People

Among the Haida, the canoe people are spirit beings who travel perpetually among the islands, appearing ashore whenever a shaman opens the way. Before this first occurred they did not realize they were spirits or who they were.

> Then they set off, they say.
> After they had travelled a ways,
> a wren sang to one side of them.
> They could see that it punctured
> a blue hole through the heart
> of the one who had passed closest to it, they say.
> > (Ghandl, "Those Who Stay a Long Way Out to Sea,"
> > trans. Robert Bringhurst.)

They're out there, the unformed ones,
shapes in sea-mist, half-
coagulated air, in their mossy
second-hand canoe. They're out there, the one
who holds the sky up, and the one who runs on
water, having no names to hang on,
old man's beard to branch, or fasten onto,
kelp to rock, or live in, hermit crab
to whelk shell. Out there,
sticking their soft canoe-nose into every cove
and inlet, the one who holds the bow pole and the
one who always bails, knowing nothing, having no raven side
and eagle side to think with, maundering their wayless way

among the islands, and now even
into English with its one-thing-then-
another-traffic-signalled syntax: out there, never
having heard their keel's bone-crunch on the beach, the terrible
birth cry of the plot, out there, the one who floats
the falcon feather, the one with bulging eyes, and the one
I almost recognize, already victim of the wren's bright
hammered music, bravely wearing in his heart that
delicate blue hole through which, I think,
he listens.

The Bushtits' Nest

When I moved to the west coast from New Brunswick, bushtits were one of the first west-of-the-Rockies species I met. Unlike most such meetings, this one did not occur with my gaze flung outward through the binoculars and my body skewed – like a violinist waiting for the downbeat or a batter for the pitch – by the effort of attentiveness. In fact I was relaxing with a drink at a friend's house when they paid us a visit – a dozen or so flitting around on the branches of the Garry oaks which overhang the porch, landing on the railing, kibitzing in true titmouse style while they visibly considered our shoulders and wine glasses as possible perches. "Ah, you're the bird watcher," Rachel said, with a troubling use of the definite article, "you can tell us what these are. They always come round when we sit out here."

Of course I couldn't – which was socially embarrassing, but at the same time exciting, since the details of their presence — those flits like precise whims, the head-cock which is both curious and skeptical, the subtle grey-brown plumage (later reduced by Roger Tory Peterson to "nondescript"), their membership in a loose, chatty klatsch that seems like an idealized version of grassroots democracy: all this could occur without the centralizing and reductive influence of the name, which so often signals the terminal point of our interest. "Ah, bushtits": check, snap. Next topic.

But naming has its indisputable satisfactions. To find bushtits later in the bird guide, to fit them ("I *knew* it") into the titmouse family along with chickadees of every stripe and cap: this is one of the pleasures of system to which us big brains are addicted. We aren't (certainly I wasn't) willing to remain on the phenomenological edge for very long before that itch to identify things, to place them taxonomically, kicks in. I'd hesitate to say that satisfactions of naming are erotic ones, but they certainly come with the sense of a compulsion relieved — akin to smoking, maybe, or finding a washroom when the call is urgent. And knowing the name leads to other tidbits of knowledge: for instance that southwestern BC is the northern extremity of their range; that they are songless (meaning, really, that their twittering *recitative* covers the function of territory and breeding managed by a separate song in other species); and that they weave elaborate hanging nests like hairy gourds — larger and more intricate than a northern oriole's, complete with a side entrance and a roof.

I have access to all these wonders because I have passed through the strait gate of nomenclature. Of course, the field guides and reference books usually convey information in terse asyntactical bursts of fact and like to think of themselves as clinically awe-free. But the pose is pretty thin, and wears through entirely in their frequent recourse to metaphor, often, interestingly, when attempting descriptions of songs and calls. A Swainson thrush's call note ("whoit") is the sound of a drop of water in a barrel; a rose-breasted grosbeak sounds like a Robin who has been taking singing lessons. And that move into mini-poem, far from being an aberration, is often the point of greatest descriptive accuracy, when a sure sense of the song (flight, nest, whatever) is conveyed. If you're like me, that is also the point that's likely to stick in memory, long after the dates and measurements have abandoned the premises.

But I want to claim something more for these metaphorical moments, having to do with their energy, with the sheer muscle required to speak a lie in the interests of truth, and leap between two distant regions of experience. One metaphor for the excitement of metaphors is to say that they are entry points where wilderness re-invades language, the place where words put their authority at risk, implicitly confessing their inadequacy to the task of re-presenting the world. Their very excess points to a world beyond language, even while it cuts a fancy linguistic figure. They are our route back to that live, still nameless birdlet who is checking out the half-recumbent drinkers on the porch, one flit away from taking an experimental sip of my Sauvignon Blanc.

⁂

Is there any paradox more telling, more reverberant and carrying in its gesture, than the one set in motion by the first lines of the *Tao Te Ching*?

> The tao that can be told
> is not the eternal Tao.
> The name that can be named
> is not the eternal Name.
> (Trans. Stephen Mitchell)

At the outset, this disclaimer about the ability of language to do the job: it can be no more than — in the traditional metaphor — a finger pointing at the moon.

And there is also the legend of how the *Tao Te Ching* came to be written, adding the charm and acoustical dwell of anecdote. Lao-tzu, having lived for a long time in the country of Chou, was leaving. The border guard, realizing this was his last chance to consult the sage, asked for a book to teach him the way. So Lao-tzu wrote the *Tao Te Ching*, gave it to the border guard, and left.

I think about this scene quite a bit: not only the sage leaving for what I think of as wilderness — the placeless place beyond the mind's appropriations — and not only the great poem written and immediately let go; I also think of that border guard with his divided being, guarding the frontier while revering the sage whose teachings point beyond it. I think his situation quite resembles the poet's, or at least the nature poet's. Whatever her admiration for wilderness, she remains a citizen of the frontier, a creature of words who will continue to use them to point — sometimes at the moon, sometimes simply at the figure of the departed sage. A poem, or poem-in-waiting, contemplates what language can't do: then it does something with language — in homage, or grief, or anger, or praise.

One writes because one has been touched by the yearning for and despair of ever touching the Other.
(Charles Simic, in *The Poet's Notebook*)

Naturally, one thinks of superb moments in lyric poetry as the entry points of wilderness. But even institutional language sometimes stumbles into a forlorn eloquence, possibly because the level of appropriation is so extreme that wilderness is made conspicuous, and vocal, by its absence. Most of us could point to a few suburbs and malls whose burlesque of 'natural' phenomena is classic; sometimes they're named after the very white oaks or crystal creeks lost or compromised in their construction. I was thinking along these lines while driving in the back country of southern Vancouver Island, where — as elsewhere — the logging road often takes its name from the creek or river that has, over ten thousand years or so, cut a pass into hills and provided the road with access to the cut-blocks. So if you're travelling on the Mosquito Creek Main or Harris Creek Main, you should be prepared for some fairly dismal views of the creek so named. They may also be views that are only too unobstructed, since the avowed practice of leaving a substantial fringe of trees along water courses as a stay against erosion seems to be more often ignored than honoured. Perhaps the most extreme case of such eloquence in my experience is Jordan River Main, partly because of its echo of the sacred river of the holy land, and partly because the river is — for a good portion of its length — gone. Jordan River has been dammed to generate electrical power and sent, first underground through a tunnel beneath the ridge, then overland through a penstock which crawls through a clear-cut area (where it looks like a leftover prop from an extremely low budget sci-fi flick about cosmic worms) before it is finally discharged through the turbines and allowed to flow out into the Strait of Juan de Fuca. Matériel. So views of Jordan River from Jordan River Main or Jordan River East Main are in fact views of the basaltic boulders which were once its bed. Name as epitaph.

A SMALL FABLE

It had been a long hard day, but he had performed perfectly, a parade of A-pluses. Every suggestion he made had been endorsed 100 percent by his proud parent, and set instantly in bronze. But that night he woke up troubled. The shadow of doubt which had lent just the right dark note to the noontide ceremony, the hint of a minor key, had now become the prevailing mood. Adam played over his choices — otter, egret, archaeopteryx, columbine, yellow warbler, zebra — trying to recall that immense mid-day satisfaction, that sense of an inexorable order inexorably ordering, as though his Father's gaze had simply entered the creature to gaze back. "Onion," said the onions; "Trumpeter swan," said the trumpeter swans; "Enchanter's nightshade," said the enchanter's nightshades with — was that the suggestion of a smirk? Surely not. But now Adam was not sure he hadn't missed something, some slippage in the belts and snaps, a little play between "Cooper's hawk" and the bird with the fierce orange eye and the talons like sharpened knitting needles. It bothered him; he got up and began to prowl around the bower, fidgeting, plucking at the odd fig leaf, his mind already hatching the idea of a cigarette and a cup of coffee.

From outside came a sad shaking of the air, a small whinny which Adam knew to be the voice of the screech owl he had named at 4:37 that afternoon. *Screech* owl? What had he been thinking? Obviously by 4:30 his edge was off and it had been clear that his Father would endorse any old label just to keep things, as He liked to say, on sched. Now Adam could see — or rather hear — what a bonehead of a name it was. Anyone could tell you that a screech was an *ascending* scream: his mind flashed forward to a '58 Pontiac Bonneville braking, *screeching* into the rending metal crash and tinkling of glass which followed. But the owl's voice fluttered down, a heart sinking, it went down like — Adam paused, finger to lips — like a little aluminum ladder. Bingo. This was more like it: "the little aluminum ladder of its scream." Adam loved its riskiness, its resonance, the way it connected something airy with the world of tools and — incredibly — found common ground. How it made the etched, metallic quality of the owl's call come forward; how it made the ladder into an act. The resonances just kept oscillating, unlike "screech owl," which just sat there, glum, a cage for the bird which could be set down in one place or another in the sentence. Adam thought of calling his Father to propose a revision, but he could already hear the note of disapproval in His voice at the suggestion of spending six words on what was after all one of Creation's smaller owls. Adam remembered His stern gaze, His dislike of shilly-shallying, His love of code.

By this time sleep had withdrawn for the night (so recently separated from the day) and Adam was thoroughly agitated. He recalled his nominations with a new critical eye and ear, feeling their clunkiness, their prefab quality: ring-necked duck, common loon: they lay there like shucked cocoons. He walked outside, and down the path toward the woods. Most things were shapes that loomed or withdrew into pools of darkness, and nothing wore the label it had been given that afternoon. Was that red oak? Was that silver maple? Adam approached, hoping to embrace a trunk, and got jabbed just below the eye by a stiff twig covered in needles. "Black spruce" he remembered, quickly amending to "bristling boreal arms." Would the whole ceremony have to be done again under the moon's changing eye? Would everything have to have a day name and a night name?

Suddenly he felt, rather than saw or heard, a stirring as a presence flew past him, a darker darkness that swept down the path and into the foliage, leaving a little whinny hanging. That was "little aluminum ladder of its scream" alright, but now Adam realized that the new name, much though it improved on "screech owl," did nothing for that gentle fatal presence on the path, that extra hush he had lived with for a moment. It was as if — Adam groped inwardly as he made his way back to the bower, holding the quality of the experience in his mind as though cradling an egg. It was as if ...

Would it be later that night, or the next day, or very much later after sex and the fall, that he'd finally name that presence on the path as the little sister of death? Or would that be one of those that never came to words?

His beak could open a bottle,
and his eyes — when he lifts their soft lids —
go on reading something
just beyond your shoulder —
Blake, maybe,
or the Book of Revelation.

Never mind that he eats only
the black-smocked crickets,
and dragonflies if they happen

to be out late over the ponds, and of course
the occasional festal mouse.
Never mind that he is only a memo
from the offices of fear —

it's not size but surge that tells us
when we're in touch with something real,
and when I hear him in the orchard
fluttering
down the little aluminum ladder of his scream —
(from Mary Oliver's "Little Owl
Who Lives in the Orchard.")

The *duende* of Lorca: a violent upsurge of the other inside language and art — the arrival of chthonic force with its irrationality, its earthiness, its message that death is just *there*, at your elbow; the dread connection to wilderness along the dark artery of our common mortality. And the 'animal music' of Ted Hughes, that vestige of shamanic power in poetry which can "make the spirits listen," and can, unless regulated and domesticated by the forms of art, induce madness.

With idea, sound, or gesture, the duende enjoys fighting the creator on the very rim of the well. Angel and muse escape with violin, meter and compass; the duende wounds. In the healing of that wound, which never closes, lies the strange, invented qualities of a man's work.

> (Federico Garcia Lorca, "Play and Theory in the Duende")

And Hughes:

> Like that cry within the sea,
> A mumbling over and over
> Of ancient law, the phrasing falling to pieces
> Garbled among shell-shards and gravels,
>   the truth falling to pieces,
>
> The sea pulling everything to pieces
> Except its killers, alert and shapely
>
>   (from "Logos")

What a contrast to the crossings recommended and demonstrated by the Taoist sages! In the exercise of spontaneity, or the knack that animates craft (cooking, pottery, archery, music), the border simply vanishes and wilderness, unfettered by consciousness, expresses itself.

> The poem makes itself
> when it is ready and the poet
> light-hearted enough in his grief
> or good fortune
>
> In the valley below Filloti
> we had our lunch under an oak tree,
> the wind blowing the paper on
> which I cut bread
>
> (John Steffler, "Wind")

> Culture can, first, be interpreted ... as an intention to remove the *otherness* of Nature, which, alien and previous, surprises and strikes the immediate identity that is the Same of the human self.
>
> (Emmanuel Levinas, "The Philosophical Determination of the Idea of Culture," *Entre Nous*)

It is the legacy of Emmanuel Levinas' thought that we should be able to contemplate the other as a fundamental category, to dislodge our usual assumptions about the primacy of such things as sameness, selfhood, ego, being and totality. No less than Lorca or Hughes, Levinas realizes how the self defends its identity against incursions of wilderness (the 'alien and previous' otherness of Nature) by the complicated apparatus of culture, which works to reinforce those very assumptions. But this set of centralizing tendencies leads both to the distortion of reality and to the related political evils of totality. The contrary idea of wholeness, with otherness kept scrupulously in mind, Levinas calls infinity.

For Levinas, ethics — which we might summarize as the calling-into-question of our freedom to control, process, or reduce the other — should be 'first philosophy'; that is, it is with ethics, and not ontology (as with Heidegger) that we should begin our attempts to understand the world. Heidegger, in whose philosophy Levinas was initially immersed, had proposed ontology — the philosophy of being — as first philosophy, itself replacing or "overcoming" the metaphysics which, Heidegger claimed, had dominated western philosophy since Aristotle.

And Heidegger is also known for what seems at first glance to be the excellent advice that we should 'let beings be', rather than reducing them to the status of 'standing reserve', as, for example, cut-blocks or kidnapped rivers. But Levinas calls this into question. Is it sufficient simply to leave the other alone, to take a hands-off position?

> Is our relation to the other a *letting be*? Is not the independence of the other achieved through his or her rôle as one who is addressed? Is the person to whom we speak understood beforehand in his being? Not at all. The other is not first an object of understanding and then an interlocutor. The two relations are merged. In other words, addressing the other is inseparable from understanding the other.
>
> <div align="right">("Is Ontology Fundamental?", <i>Entre Nous</i>)</div>

A person might be reminded here of Wittgenstein's remark that meaning is going up to someone. This view of the importance of *address* to the other (as opposed to passivity or 'letting beings be'), with its implication that the gesture acknowledges a responsibility, a limitation of the freedom of beings in favour of the other, reaches a point of dramatic focus in Levinas' concept of the Face.

What Levinas means by the Face is, I think, the other encountered in a relationship of address and discovered to be quite untranslatable into systems of sameness and linguistic organization; it is foreign-ness that remains foreign, always exceeding our categories of knowing, always "over and beyond form" (*Totality and Infinity*). It seems to be a far more nuanced, philosophically literate and conceptually far-reaching version of what I've been calling wilderness, as this expresses itself in poetic attention.

But a problem presents itself — at least for me — and, interestingly, it is a problem of nomenclature. To personify the untranslated other as the Face seems, in fact, to translate it into terms which are, if not exclusively human, at least composed largely of members of the 'higher' animal kingdom, shutting out such creatures as Douglas-fir, waves and clams, to say nothing of lichens, rocks and chairs. Its strength lies in its appeal to the experience we often have of 'putting a face' to another person, or 'recognizing' the rights and values of a minority group. It is easier, probably even for a Texas governor, to kill an abstract criminal on death row than a person whose face one has seen in photographs or the flesh. But in its apparent anthropocentrism (or vertebratocentrism?), the Face initially seems an inadequate term for any non-animal other we might truly address.

But further reflection may reveal, as it did for me, something of the wisdom of Levinas' choice. Anthropocentrism, in Walt Disney films or plans for wildlife management, may be an evil we wish to avoid. But when we take stock of our situation as language users with brains and organs of perception which dictate that we see and describe the world in human ways, we can see that, at bottom, a human perspective is impossible to escape. Though we may devote attention to the screech owl or the cat-tail moss, we are inevitably translators of their being, at least when we come to representation. "Isn't art," Levinas asks rhetorically, "an activity that gives things a face?" Even an artist like Cézanne, whose work, as Merleau-Ponty puts it, renders a perspective "from below the imposed order of humanity" as if "viewed by a creature of another species," has not truly managed to escape the perspectival cage. How could he, given the huge inheritance of pigment, canvas, frame, and so forth? But what he does manage to do, and dramatically, is make us aware that the cage exists.

So here's how I'm reading the Face: it's an address to the other with an acknowledgement of our human-centredness built in, a salutary and humbling reminder. We can perform artistic acts in such a way that, in 'giving things a face' the emphasis falls on the gift, the way, for example, a linguistic community might honour a stranger by conferring upon her a name in their language. Homage is, perhaps, simply appropriation with the current reversed; 'here', we say to the thing, 'is a tribute from our culture, in which having a face is the premier sign of status.' We can, in short, try to be like Cézanne rather than Mount Rushmore.

STOOL

In the end one cannot keep this love concealed
tiny quadruped with oaken legs
o skin coarse and fresh beyond expression
everyday object eyeless but with a face
on which the wrinkles of the grain mark a ripe judgement
grey little mule most patient of mules
its hair has fallen out from too much fasting
and only a tuft of wooden bristle
can my hand feel when I stroke it in the morning

— Do you know my darling they were charlatans
who said: the hand lies the eye
lies when it touches shapes that are empty —

they were bad people envious of things
they wanted to trap the world with the bait of denial

how to express to you my gratitude wonder
you come always to the call of the eye
with great immobility explaining by dumb-signs
to a sorry intellect: we are genuine —
At last the fidelity of things opens our eyes

(Zbigniew Herbert, trans. Czeslaw Milosz & Peter Dale Scott)

Envisaging rather than naming: to bring in all that a face presents – character, expression, imagination, mobility of feature, traces of the past in lines and crowfeet. A face is a face is a face; it is not primarily a linguistic being whose chief virtue is ease of manipulation. And when a lake or a pine marten looks back, when we are – however momentarily – *vis à vis*, the pause is always electric. Are we not right to sense, in such meetings, that envisaging flows both ways?

> How the slash looks: not
> ruin, abattoir, atrocity;
> not harvest, regen, working
> forest. How it looks. The way it
> keeps on looking when we look away,
> embarrassed. How it gawks,
> with no nuance or subterfuge
> or shadow. How it seems to see us now
> as we see it. Not quick.
> Not dead.

Last spring, while out watching for returning warblers in a local park, I came upon a pair of bushtits building their nest. Actually, I didn't realize what they were doing right off: it seemed like some sort of bonding ritual in which each of them buzzed from the surrounding trees into this one open space at the top of a dogwood shrub, fluttered a moment, then buzzed out again. Unlike their usual flitterings, these flights were filled with intent; aimed. Eventually I was able to make out something in that space, some slight thickening of air, if it wasn't one of those gauzy jellyfish-like floaters that can occur in your vision due to some momentary aberration inside your eyeball. The bushtits were — as I inferred later with the help of reference books — probably just beginning to attach leaf matter and lichens to the spider web they use for struts and girders (and which apparently has tensile strength greater than steel), but to me it looked like their flitterings were an attempt to summon something out of nothing, preparing the air for some sudden incarnation. When I went back the next day the nest already had the consistency of a string bag or a cloud of algae, and its gourd shape was visible. The bushtits continued to buzz in and out, only now I could see the occasional bit of twig or leaf in their beaks, and they would land on one of the adjacent branches before tucking the new bit into the nest-in-progress.

In this passage, it is useful to remember that for the ancient Chinese, the heart is the organ of thought.

> 'I venture to enquire about the fasting of the heart.'
>
> 'Unify your attention. Rather than listen with the ear, listen with the heart. Rather than listen with the heart, listen with the energies. Listening stops at the ear, the heart at what tallies with the thought. As for energy [Chi] it is the tenuous which waits to be roused by other things. Only the Way accumulates the tenuous. The attenuating is the fasting of the heart.'
> (Chuang-tzu, *The Seven Inner Chapters*, trans. A.C. Graham)

To be next door to nothing: it's not only their nests, but the bushtits themselves that convey this paradoxical power. They are 'creatures of the air' not only because they fly through it, but because it comprises so much of their bodily presence. All birds, in fact, live close to the edge. Typically, they draw air into sacs throughout their bodies, and even, in some cases, into their hollow bones. They also expel all the air from the lungs with each exhalation, without holding back, as we do, a reserve. Nor do they put on fat they aren't about to burn up in migration. Birds do not need a Lao-tzu to remind them of the non-being their lives depend on.

It was a while after I observed the bushtits in the park that I noticed similar busyness in the forsythia bush which hangs over our driveway. Sure enough, another pair had chosen this improbable space eighteen inches over a Toyota Corolla, with its door slams and exhaust, its big blocky comings and goings, as the site of their future home. I think the forsythia's tangle of twigs and branches may have appealed to them as stabilizers coming to the assistance of spider webs. At first, I was careful not to park in the driveway for fear of disturbing them, but – having forgotten once or twice – it soon became apparent that the bushtits' idea of home was closer to a kitchen in Newfoundland than to a hermitage. The car didn't bother them, and neither, it seemed, did our curiosity, which – after all – seemed to echo theirs.

Now, eight months later, the bushtits have long since raised their chicks and left, but the forsythia tangle still holds this gathered thickness inside it, looking like a vital organ. It is easy to stand in the driveway and inspect it close up – an infinity of tucks and weavings worked in grasses, mosses and lichens. Cat-tail moss seems to have been especially useful for its feather boa-like length and softness, and so has one of the beard lichens (*Usnea subfloridana?*), which has a strong central cord like a tendon running through it. I think the lichens came largely from our neighbour's wood fence, where at least four species grow in profusion, and where I have often seen bushtits perching – briefly – in a pause between flits.

Since moving to BC and meeting a bona fide lichenologist in the person of Trevor Goward, I've become aware of just how abundant and amazing these overlooked beings are. That is not the sort of awareness anyone who meets Trevor is likely to escape, since his commitment to 'the spread of enlichenment', as he puts it, is intense. He would certainly want it noted that the bushtits have been engaged in the reproduction of lichens while they are busy about reproduction of their own, since those lichens that do not spread through spores rely on the transportation of bits of their thalluses (bodies) by birds. But more fundamentally, he would want us to realize that a lichen is a very complex life form, the visible consequence of a symbiotic relationship between a fungus and microscopic algae. Lichens are, in Trevor's memorable and – at least among the enlichened – famous metaphor, fungi that have discovered agriculture.

I remember reading that phrase in the lichen section of

Plants of Coastal British Columbia before I met its author, and being immediately engaged. Thinking back to that experience will provide a convenient place to end (though not to conclude), since it returns us to the scene of naming and envisaging we've been busily flitting around, tucking and weaving. Besides the elegance of Trevor's metaphor, and the efficiency with which it does the job of informing, we should notice the implied homage or gift that the gesture makes: to see lichens as fungi that practice agriculture is to see them in the same light that we conceive our own passage, as human beings, from the raw to the cooked, and to confer on them some of the value and acclaim we usually reserve for things human. And while we're paused there, mildly agog at the prospect of domestication occurring in the natural world, let's also take in the pure pizzazz of the metaphorical act releasing another micro-quantum of wild figuration into the body of language – that tiny, shocking, necessary invasion; that saving of language from itself.

Sources

Some of these essays and poems have previously appeared in slightly different form: "Baler Twine: Thoughts on Ravens, Home and Nature Poetry" is reprinted from *Poetry and Knowing* with the permission of Quarry Press; "Matèriel" is reprinted from Don McKay's *Apparatus* with the permission of McClelland & Stewart, Ltd., The Canadian Publishers; and "Remembering Apparatus: Poetry and the Visibility of Tools" first appeared in *Queens Quarterly*. Quotations found throughout the text are from the following sources (listed in order of appearance):

BALER TWINE

Berger, John. *And our faces, my heart, brief as photos.* New York: Pantheon, 1984.
Neruda, Pablo Neruda. *Isla Negra.*. Trans. Alistair Reid. New York: Farrar Straus and Giroux, 1981.

REMEMBERING APPARATUS

McLuhan, Marshall. *Understanding Media.* New York: Signet, 1964.
Ullman, Ellen. *Resisting the Virtual Life.* Ed. James Brook. San Francisco: City Lights, 1998.

Zwicky, Jan. "Language is Hands." *The New Room*. Toronto: Coach House, 1989.
Neruda, Pablo. *Still Another Day*. Port Townsend: Copper Canyon, 1984.
de Man, Paul. "The Epistemology of Metaphor." *Critical Inquiry*. 5.1 (1978) and *On Metaphor*. Ed. Sheldon Sacks. Chicago: U of Chicago, 1978.
Nietzsche, Friedrich. "On Truth and Lies in an Extra-Moral Sense." *The Portable Nietzsche*. Ed. Walter Kaufmann. New York: Penguin, 1968.

THE CANOE PEOPLE

Ghandl of the Qayahl Laanas. *Nine Visits to the Mythworld*. Trans. Robert Bringhurst. Vancouver and Toronto: Douglas and McIntyre, 2000.

THE BUSHTITS' NEST

Tao Te Ching. trans. Stephen Mitchell. New York: Harper Collins, 1991.
Simic, Charles. *The Poet's Notebook*. Ed. Stephen Kuuisto et al. New York: Norton, 1995.
Oliver, Mary. "Little Owl Who Lives in the Orchard." *New and Selected Poems*. Boston: Beacon Press, 1992.
Lorca, Federico Garcia. "Play and Theory in Duende." *In Search of Duende*. New York: New Directions, 1998.
Hughes, Ted Hughes. "Logos." *Wodwo*. London: Faber and Faber, 1967.
Steffler, John. "Wind." *That Night We Were Ravenous*. Toronto: McClelland and Stewart, 1998.
Levinas, Emmanuel. "The Philosophical Determination of the Idea of Culture." *Entre Nous*. Trans. Michael B. Smith and Barbara Harshav. London: Athlone, 1998.
—. "Is Ontology Fundamental?" *Entre Nous*. Trans. Michael B. Smith and Barbara Harshav. London: Athlone, 1998.
Merleau-Ponty, Maurice. "Cezanne's Doubt." *The Essential Merleau-Ponty*. Ed. Alden Fisher. New York: Harcourt Brace, 1969.

Herbert, Zbigniew. "Stool." Trans. Czeslaw Milosz and Peter Dale Scott. New York: Ecco Press, 1968.

Changu-tzu. *The Seven Inner Chapters and other writings*. Trans A.C. Graham. London: George Allen and Unwin, 1981.

Text copyright © Don McKay, 2001.
Illustrations copyright © Wesley W. Bates, 2001.

All rights reserved. No part of this publication may be reproduced in any form without the prior written consent of the publisher. Any requests for the photocopying of any part of this book should be directed in writing to the Canadian Copyright Licensing Agency.

This book was typeset in Adobe Centaur by Andrew Steeves and printed offset by Gary Dunfield at Gaspereau Press. Printed on Synergy natural laid, an acid-free paper made from fifty percent recycled fibre.

Gaspereau Press acknowledges the support of the Canada Council for the Arts and the Nova Scotia Department of Tourism and Culture for its publishing program.

1   3   5   4   2

CANADIAN CATALOGUING IN PUBLICATION DATA

McKay, Don, 1942–
Vis à vis: fieldnotes on poetry and wilderness

Essays and poems.
ISBN 1-894031-51-2 (BOUND)
ISBN 1-894031-50-4 (PBK.)

1. Poetry.   2. Nature in literature.   I. Title.
PS8575.K28V58 2001   C811'.54   C2001-902366-9
PR9199.3.M323V58 2001

GASPEREAU PRESS
POST OFFICE BOX 143
WOLFVILLE, NOVA SCOTIA
CANADA B0P 1X0